Copyright@-2022-A.J Robbie Lyna

Contents

HOW I ALSO BECAME RICH IN BABYLON

Best Guide To Financial Success

By

A.J Robbie Lyna

PART ONE: PLANNING

INVESTMENT

ACCUMULATION

We're going to talk about wealth accumulation. Specifically, ideas for how to accumulate wealth and accumulate wealth faster. If you have read the book The Millionaire Next Door you'll recall that they spend a lot of time comparing Prodigious Accumulators of Wealth (PAW's) and Under Accumulators of Wealth (UAW's). My goal for all of you is to become

Prodigious Accumulators of Wealth so

you can achieve financial independence

sooner

Without further ado, let's dive into tips

for rapid wealth accumulation!

CHAPTER 1:PAY YOURSELF FIRST

The term has been used before.First, pay yourself.Before you spend money, be sure to put it toward your goals.

Monetary arranging can be summarized in eight words: buckle down, spend a bit, contribute the distinction. However, i like to switch that request up. Buckle down, contribute a ton, spend the distinction.

In the event that you are taking care of a satisfactory sum to accomplish your monetary objectives in the time period you need to accomplish them, go crazy on spending the rest! Try not to have a messy outlook on it, all things considered! Your objectives are on target!

Disregard planning to keep your spending all together. Center around coordinating satisfactory sums towards your different monetary objectives, like retirement, school investment funds, and so on, and let your costs top off the rest. In the event that you burn through cash first, you'll find it trying to think of sufficient cash to contribute towards your abundance gathering objectives.

Definition and Examples of a Pay-Yourself-First Budget

A compensation yourself-first financial plan is an opposite planning procedure where you save a piece of your pay first — basically dealing with your reserve funds like a bill — then utilize the remainder of your cash to cover expenses and spend anyway you see fit.

Substitute name: Reverse financial plan Because you don't have to spend time tracking your costs, a compensation yourself-first financial plan is simpler than other types of spending plans.You'll be fine as long as you focus on reserve funds, pay your bills, and avoid taking on more debt.

For instance, suppose you want to save 20% of your pay. So you save 10% for retirement, 5% in a backup stash, and 5% in a get-away asset. Presently, you can uninhibitedly spend the other 80% on needs and needs.

"My favored planning strategy is opposite planning," said R.J. Weiss, a guaranteed monetary organizer and pioneer behind The Ways to Wealth. "This technique is the point at which you're paying your objectives first (e.g., investment funds, travel store, house up front installment, and so on) and afterward you're ready to spend what's extra. Along these lines, one deals with their objectives, preferably through

programmed moves, and afterward can

unreservedly spend what's extra."

CHAPTER 2: MAKE INVESTING MORE EVERY YEAR A GOAL

If you want to rapidly accumulate wealth, make it a goal to increase the amount you invest each and every year. If you invested 20% of your income in 2021, try to invest 22% in 2022. If you invested $75,000 for your retirement goals last year, try to invest $80,000 this year.

Contribute the majority of any reward or salary increase you receive and maintain your current spending level..

Track your investment funds rate consistently and make it a contest with yourself to save more this year than you did the year before. Small step your direction to increasingly high abundance amassing.

To gather abundance quicker, put forth a strong attempt to keep on developing the cash stack at a rising rate.

A compensation yourself-first financial plan works precisely as it sounds: You reserve your investment funds objectives first, then, at that point, you utilize the remainder of your check anyway you like. While there are many advantages to this sort of financial plan, there likewise are disadvantages to know about.

Here is a more critical gander at how a compensation yourself-first financial plan works so you can choose if it's the best technique for you.

Our relationship with cash begins at an early age when we notice relatives trading coins or bills for a wide range of stuff we like. Cash's power and authority develop when we get our most memorable recompense or paid errand. These early encounters encourage propensities and convictions that last all through your life. Its difficulties duplicate as we approach adulthood and are urged to take credits to pay for school or purchase a vehicle.

Parental figures set the vibe for venture objectives from the get-go throughout everyday life, training us to defer satisfaction until we can break the stash, permitting those coins to purchase computer games, garments or hardware. The personal association among venture and way of life develops more modern as the years pass. The finish of your functioning life is either an agreeable retirement - or a battle to earn enough to get by.

How Life and Investment Goals Intersect

Age, pay, and point of view determine the three branches of the venture's goals.Age can be further broken down into three distinct categories:young and just starting out, moderately old and building a family, and old and independent.These groups frequently fail to leave their mark on the appropriate era, such as when people in the Middle Ages looked at speculations with interest or when older people were forced to carefully budget, practicing the discipline they needed as young adults.

Pay gives the regular beginning stage to venture objectives since you can't contribute what you don't have. The principal vocation work gives a reminder for the vast majority youngsters, constraining choices around 401(k) commitments, investment funds or currency market records and way of life changes expected to offset developing riches with postponed delight. It's not unexpected to encounter difficulties during this period, stalling out in overrated home rental and vehicle installments or failing to remember that your watchmen are done getting the month to month MasterCard bill. Viewpoint portrays the battleground on which we work during our lifetimes and our decisions that influence abundance the board. Family arranging dwells at the first spot on the list for the vast majority, with couples concluding the number of children they that need, their favored areas and the number of workers will be expected to match those objectives.

Profession assumptions dovetail into these estimations, with the profoundly taught sloping into long stretches of expanded profit power while others are trapped in impasse occupations, compelled to scale back to earn barely enough to get by.

Venture objectives become moving focuses for some people, with painstakingly spread out plans running into road obstructions as cutbacks,

impromptu pregnancies, medical

problems and the need to really focus on

maturing guardians. Those startling

difficulties request a portion of

authenticity while picking 401(k)

designations or choosing how to spend a

year-end reward, with the familiar

maxim "keeping for later" disregarded by

numerous people until it's past the point

of no return.

Luckily, turning into an investor is rarely

past the point of no return. You might be

in your 40s prior to understanding that

life is moving surprisingly rapidly,

requiring consideration about retirement.

Dread can rule your reasoning assuming you stand by this long to define venture objectives, yet that is OK on the off chance that it adds a need to get going to abundance the board. All ventures start with the principal dollar put away for that reason, whatever your age, pay, or viewpoint. Obviously, those effective financial planning for a really long time hold a significant benefit, while their developing abundance permits them to partake in the products of their saving propensities.

SET UP AN INVESTMENT GOALS WORKFLOW

Speculation objectives address three significant topics with respect to cash and cash the executives. In the first place, they converge with a day to day existence plan that draws in our perspectives surprisingly. Second, they produce responsibility, constraining us to survey progress on an occasional premise, conjuring discipline when expected to keep focused. Third, they produce inspiration that influences our non-monetary selves in certain ways that can further develop well-being and mental viewpoint.

When laid out, the growth strategy drives you to believe about penances that should be made and spending plans that should be adjusted, understanding that deferral or disappointment will promptly affect your riches and way of life. This cycle prompts long-range thinking and arranging, permitting you to leave a hand-to-mouth approach and put forth a boundary list for the things in life you genuinely esteem.

Utilize month to month or quarterly proclamations to audit progress and commit once again to your picked life plan, making little changes instead of enormous changes when cash stream improves or decays. Survey your yearly returns intermittently, and appreciate seeing your abundance develop without direct intercession or an occasion check from a family member. Figure out how to manage losing periods in a developed way, utilizing the red ink to construct persistence while reevaluating what your navigation might have meant for those negative returns.

The Australian Investors Association recommends using the SMART format when setting investment goals.

Specific – make each goal clear and specific

Measurable – frame each goal so that you know when you have achieved it

Achievable – you need to take practical action to achieve a goal

Relevant – determine whether your goals relate to your life and are realistic

Time-based – assign a time frame to each goal so you can track progress

Start by writing a document or journal that lists each investment goal and how you'll measure progress. List as much detail as possible, considering both short-term and long-term objectives. Let's say you want to save for retirement but also plan to own a home in a safe

neighborhood, with enough cash left over

for an occasional vacation. Now review

your current financial situation, noting

how well you've handled money to this

point and the steps you're willing to take

to achieve that list of goals.

It very well might be untimely to

consider the pragmatic activities required

or time periods expected to stamp

progress assuming your speculation

objectives are unreasonable, abnormal or

don't match your current or expected

profit power. You can dream about

satisfying life's longings, however

speculation arranging requires a ruthless

rude awakening prior to executing the required activity plan. Just expressed, on the off chance that the arrangement doesn't match your existence or your objectives, discard it and begin once again. Focus on gradual steps as opposed to wide brush fantasizes.

A little 401(k) commitment might be all that is required to get the money growth strategy on target during its early stages. Bosses here and there match your commitment to a specific level, which permits you to contemplate more modern arranging in the long run. Monetary counsels suggest you dispense the most extreme permitted whenever the situation allows albeit that is unreasonable for the vast majority youngsters simply beginning in their vocations. This is particularly obvious with the gigantic weight of educational loans brought about by individuals brought into the world after 1990.

CHAPTER 3

:MANAGING TIME

FRAMES

Break speculation objectives into short-, moderate and long haul fragments while conceivable, matching the normal life phases of youth, middle age and post-retirement years. Adjusting bank and investment funds to short and middle terms additionally appears to be legit while retirement accounts center solely around the long haul (firm punishments are brought about while getting to those assets rashly). As a matter of fact, there's not a great explanation to take advantage of IRAs, SEP and other retirement accounts except if desperate conditions offer no reasonable other options. Short-and moderate term objectives help SMART preparation too, permitting a fast survey to measure reserve funds progress for a home, vehicle, get-away, or family commitments. Halfway term arranging can likewise incorporate a more summed up account, indicating the capital put away for the unavoidable "blustery day." This secret stash distribution can likewise act as a firewall between life's shocks and the a lot bigger retirement account, permitting that money to be left immaculate, set to satisfy its planned reason.

Try not to surrender assuming that you've arrived at middle age without speculation arranging since significant advantages build rapidly when the errand is first locked in. Obviously, playing get up to speed will be required in the event that your funds are blazing red ink, requiring way of life changes until your pay coordinates or surpasses costs.

Obligation the executives will be expected to get in good shape since it's a horrible idea to procure 5% or 10% yearly in a venture account when different charge cards have hit their cutoff points at 18%, 20%, or 25% loan fees.

Figuring out how to put resources into middle age has the advantage of involvement - that is, you can all the more precisely check your future income power by inspecting the family's ongoing vocation directions. It's generally expected feasible for high-breadwinners to play make up for lost time, creating venture financial momentum rapidly in these conditions, however requiring sacrifices is still possible. Unfortunately, pay frequently deteriorates through middle age, with impasse occupations and hindered professions keeping some fortunate family funds above water

however forestalling the structure of

additional significant investment funds.

Whenever the situation allows,

retirement records ought to be

completely financed through middle age

and straight up to the furthest limit of

business in any event, when it powers

other way of life changes. Monetary

weights are probably going to increment

over the long haul, because of rising

medical care and youngster raising

expenses (which might incorporate

schooling cost). Entering retirement with

minimal more than government checks

close by can deliver very much

established uneasiness, particularly when one life partner has been subject to the next for quite a long time, and ought to be stayed away from no matter what. More people are working past retirement age now than whenever in the previous hundred years. Nonetheless, government decides expect that financial backers begin to pull out assets from retirement accounts (other than Roth IRAs) at age 70½.

 Alongside longer futures, this prerequisite adds new importance to speculation arranging in the retirement years. It seems OK for individuals beyond 70 years old to proceed with their growing long term financial stability through work or venture straight up to death whenever the situation allows, particularly on the off chance that a life partner will depend on the assets.

PART 2: NUTS AND BOLTS OF INVESTMENTS

CHAPTER 4: THE AMOUNT DO YOU NEED TO SAVE?

Monetary counsels utilize various measurements to work out retirement needs. Many recommend clients aggregate an adequate number of reserve funds during their functioning lives to supplant 70-85% of pre-retirement pay. Some even prescribe 100 percent or more to create the capital expected to seek after a side interest or travel. These normal methodologies might be obsolete, given the blast of children of post war

America staying in the work force after age 65 or 66, frequently taking compensation cuts.

Devotion Investments suggests saving something like 1x your pre-retirement pay at age 30, 3x at 40, 7x at 55 and 10x at 67. In the event that you think you'll require $100,000 each year after you resign, you ought to have $100,000 in reserve funds at age 30, $300,000 at age 40, etc. These proposals accept that clients will save 15% of their yearly pay consistently beginning at age 25, with over half of those investment funds assigned to values.

 All things considered, numerous

youngsters don't have that degree of extra

cash at age 25 because of educational

loan responsibilities or temporary

positions, and that implies a higher

yearly responsibility will be expected at a

later beginning date.

Retirement arranging might be difficult

for youngsters to achieve, yet it's

generally simple to envision the post-

work a long time with a self-assessment

that considers their normal way of life

and how they should go through their

time on earth investment funds. The

Employee Benefit Research Institute

(EBRI) makes that reflective assignment

more straightforward with its Consumption Activities and Mail Survey (CAMS), illustrating how Americans beyond 70 years old spend their cash and how those allotments change through the senior years.

Lodging costs surpassed any remaining classifications overwhelmingly, holding at 31-36% across all age gatherings. Of course, medical services costs begin somewhat little - 7% at age 45 - and beyond twofold to 15.5% at ages 75 and up. Taken together, it's normal you'll ultimately spend over half of your retirement dollars simply remaining alive and keeping a rooftop over your head.

Presently envision that it is so

challenging to meet those straightforward

requirements assuming pay is restricted

to a month to month Social Security

check. Sadly, a great many Americans

currently face that life-sobering test since

they couldn't lay out and address their

speculation objectives prior throughout

everyday life.

The orientation hole makes it harder for

ladies to accomplish retirement

objectives than men, as per research firm

Aon Hewitt. Its 2016 investigation

discovered that 83% of U.S. ladies

weren't saving enough for retirement,

contrasted with 74% of men. They gauge

that a lady will require 11.5 times her last pay to meet her retirement needs, contrasted with 10.6 times for a man. Aon Hewitt further ventures that ladies need to work a year longer, to mature 69, to make up the setback. Ladies' more drawn out life ranges heighten this retirement hole, with their reserve funds required for additional years.

These numbers are particularly disturbing on the grounds that, as the review notes, people take part in 401(k) plans at a similar 79% rate, yet ladies put away a normal 7.5% of their compensation while men designate a normal 8.7%, a shortfall exacerbated by ladies' below procuring power. In 2015, 401(k) balances for ladies were only 59% of the men's aggregate - $71,060 versus $119,150.

While the creators propose plan changes to energize higher saving rates, this dissimilarity is probably going to go on as long as the work environment orientation hole in pay remains.

CHAPTER 5:

INSTRUCTIONS TO OVERCOME INVESTMENT OBSTACLES

A recent report on objective setting by Dr. Gail Matthews, a specialist at Dominican University of California in San Rafael, reasoned that members matured 23 to 72 who set up their objectives as a written record and sent ordinary advancement reports to companions had a "a lot higher achievement rate than the people who hushed up about their objectives." as a matter of fact, over 70% of members who recorded on paper and shared their objectives revealed achievement contrasted with 35% of the people who remained quiet about their objectives, never thinking of them down.

This is a momentous finding, straightforwardly pertinent to accomplishing venture objectives and targets, offering an ideal way for people lacking discipline or resolve to beat those shortfalls in a life getting updated way. Age variety among members likewise lets us know it's never past the point where it is possible to accomplish

sensible speculation objectives for

however long we're willing to exceed

everyone's expectations, thinking of them

exhaustively and revealing our

advancement to a supportive outsider.

Obviously, even focused people might

find it hard to remain on monetary track

when life tosses a hardball toward them.

Employment cutback, separate, disorder,

segregation, or different headwinds can

set life on a surprising course that

adversely influences income and

investment funds power. Unpredictability

can likewise negatively affect the

monetary business sectors and your

reserve funds, as they did in 2007 and 2008 when American financial backers lost trillions of dollars in their retirement accounts.

Bear markets and declines might be inescapable throughout the long term between your most memorable commitment and retirement age, in spite of measurements that affirm amazing long haul value returns. Numerous financial backers don't have the stomach for those unstable periods, frequently disregarding sound counsel and unloading long haul positions at scratch and dent section costs. It's not difficult to let ourselves know we'll stand firm when the following emergency comes long, yet you won't be aware without a doubt until it works out.

Couples and Investment Goals

Pooling assets between companions offers an optimal method for beating large numbers of the difficulties presented by speculation objective setting. This approach requires profound trust on the grounds that a separation sometime down the road can have wrecking results. As per Kansas State University analyst Sonya Britt closed, "Contentions about cash (are) by a wide margin the top indicator of separation."

Two livelihoods make putting something aside for a home and fitting the bill for a home loan a lot simpler objectives to achieve. Collaboration between accomplices is essential when taken part in this middle of the road term arranging since objectives need understanding and coordination to stay away from significant complexities. One mate tapping charge card limits while the other tirelessly distributes week after week pay into investment funds can produce a significant barrier to long haul thriving. Association can likewise facilitate the lodging trouble for those ages 45 and up, when 31-36% retirement pay is apportioned to lease, contract

installments, protection, local charges

and support.

The reserve funds from pooled pay can

be huge in group oriented families,

opening up capital for different costs. On

the other hand, actual inconsistencies

between companions or accomplices

might entangle medical services costs,

with a significant sickness or institutional

consideration conquering Medicare

inclusion, making difficulty for the other

accomplice.

The Bottom Line

Sort out your venture objectives as from

the get-go in life as conceivable in light

of the fact that standing by too lengthy presents confusions that might be troublesome or difficult to survive. Arranging and execution requires a degree of discipline and responsibility that makes numerous people self-conscious, frequently requiring significant life altering events to find lasting success. Begin little in the event that the cycle feels overpowering, with least 401(k) commitments that let you watch a little retirement fund develop rapidly.

Raise the commitment to the greatest quickly and make the following stride, creating practical short-and transitional term venture objectives for the extra cash gathering in a checking or investment account. Recall this is a lifetime pursuit that requests cautious preparation at each stage, yet the result can be perfect, offering a possibly dependable way to thriving.

CHAPTER 6: DRIVE AN INEXPENSIVE CAR

To make things abundantly clear, I am not a vehicle individual. I consider a vehicle to be a method for getting you securely from point A to point B. Couldn't care less assuming the paint is scratched. Couldn't care less in the event that the seats are cowhide or material, physically or electronically change.

As well as lodging, transportation expenses can be a huge cost for a many individuals. I know certain individuals who spend more than $2,000/month in vehicle installments! $2,000/month is a ton to spend on vehicles!

If rather you paid cash for economical yet dependable vehicles one time per decade and contributed that $2,000/month, following 25 years you would have $1.2M, accepting a normal return of 5%/year. Assuming that your venture returned a normal of 7%/year, you would have $1.6M.

Speculation returns aren't ensured, obviously, and consistently is an exciting ride, yet you understand. That great vehicle you're driving could be an extra $1.5M in your savings.

By and by, I'll take more cash in the bank

over a fancier vehicle quickly.

CHAPTER 7:TRY NOT TO BUY STATUS ITEMS

The enormous house, the extravagant vehicle, the decent watch, fashioner pants; sure they look cool, yet you burned through a lot of cash on stuff. On the off chance that you burn through cash on things, you'll wind up with the things and not the cash.

You don't see abundance. Recall that next time you discover yourself attempting to stay aware of the Joneses.

The more cash you spend on the status things, the less you have accessible to contribute towards abundance aggregation.

As referenced before, put enough of your cash towards your reserve funds and speculation objectives first, and afterward spend what's extra. In the event that what's left is sufficient to purchase the status things, good luck with that.

CHAPTER 8: LIVE IN A MODEST NEIGHBORHOOD

Bringing things round trip. We began with lodging costs, so we will end with lodging costs. The auxiliary expenses of house purchasing stretch out a long ways past the home loan installment, local charges, and upkeep.

Staying aware of the Jonses is genuine. Assuming your neighbors drive decent new vehicles, have top of the line furniture, have a place with country clubs, go on rich excursions, drink costly wine, and so forth, and so on, you'll feel tension from yourself to do likewise. We need to find a place with people around us.

Then again, in the event that your neighbors wear washed-out pants, drive old vehicles, drink modest brew, and take their children setting up camp for get-away, you'll stand out in contrast to everything else in the event that you drive a great vehicle and taste pinot noir in your specially crafted teak Adirondack seat on the entryway patio.

You need to feel like you fit in with people around you. Try not to trust me? Have a go at making an appearance to a

BBQ in a suit and tie, or a to burial

service in a T-shirt and shorts and

perceive how off-kilter you feel

CHAPTER 9:BE COMFORTABLE WITH YOUR RISK

You can't get away from the fact that all investing involves a degree of risk.

Risk is defined as the probability or likelihood of occurrence of losses relative to the expected return on any particular investment.

It takes on many forms (concentration risk and liquidity risk for example).

In fact, not taking on enough is also risky itself!

In general, markets reward investors for the risk they take.

Remember, taking on more doesn't guarantee higher returns.

But if you stay invested and are able to resist the temptation to dip in and out of the market, you should eventually be rewarded for the additional risk you take. Taking risks isn't exactly fun (at least not for most people), but it's a necessary part of life. In fact, risk is pretty much built into every aspect of life. Dating is a risk, starting a new job is a risk, creating something is a risk. Anything we do that we haven't personally tried and tested presents a risk. It might work and bring us happiness and success; or it might not work, and leave us feeling like we failed. But if risk is unavoidable and necessary, how can we get more comfortable with taking risks? If there's a lot on the line, how can we overcome fear of failure and take the risks we need to take?

The value of risk

Some people are natural-born risk-takers. They challenge the status quo, stare down obstacles, and explore new possibilities and opportunities.

The rest of us (yes, us—I count myself in this group) are a little more "security-oriented." It's not that we don't respect or even admire risk-takers; it's just that we appreciate stability and comfort. It's nice to feel like you're in control, at least when it comes to some things.

The truth is, both types of people are extremely valuable to the world and society as a whole. Risk-takers change the world, and non-risk-takers keep the world safe.

But just as risk-takers need limits (i.e. they shouldn't take 100% of the risks they face, 100% of the time), non-risk-takers need to be willing to take risks from time to time.

Which begs the question: why? Why don't we all just play it safe, all the time?

Why don't we stick with what we know—the things we're good at, the things we've succeeded at before, the things we know will work? Why don't we just make the best of a situation?

Because:

Big risk can lead to big reward

While big risks can potentially lead to big disappointment, they can also lead to big rewards. If you want the payoff, you have to take the risk.

Risks lead to growth

Taking a risk will either pay off or it won't, but either way, experiences help us learn important lessons that will inform our decisions in the future.

Taking risks inspires creative thinking

When you're trying to make a risk pay off, you're likely to stretch your creative muscles to look for ways to make it work. When there's a lot at stake, you're more willing to do the creative work required to find innovative solutions that will lead you to success.

Risk reveals values

What you're willing to risk can say a lot about what you value. If you're ever trying to figure out what you really care about, think about the risks you've taken. What were you trying to gain, and what were you willing to put on the line?

Risk builds self-confidence

When risk ends in a positive way, it can boost your self confidence. When you see that your willingness to take the risk (and your willingness to put in the work to succeed) have paid off, it can give you more confidence in your decision-making abilities and creativity.

Risk helps you avoid regret

Research suggests that it's more likely that you'll regret not doing something than that you'll regret doing something, even if the thing you do doesn't go well. After all, if you never even try, you'll never know how things could have gone. In short, learning to get comfortable with taking risks can help you as you work to create the happy life you want to live. It can help you grow in meaningful ways. It can help you learn lessons you may never have learned otherwise. These rewards, and others, make risk worth…well, the risk.

"If there's even a slight chance of getting something that will make you happy, risk it. Life's too short, and happiness is too rare."

A.R. LUCAS

How to get comfortable with taking risks

Whether you're a risk-taker or not, there are some things you can to do help

yourself feel more comfortable taking
risks on a regular basis.

Develop a growth mindset

A growth mindset is all about hope, improvement, effort, and growth, rather than outcome and performance. If you have a growth mindset, you reward yourself for trying, regardless of whether or not you succeeded.

A growth mindset helps you let go of perfectionism and fear of failure. It helps you be more willing to take risks because you recognize that even if you fail, you can still learn and grow.

Developing a growth mindset is all about embracing challenges, recognizing learning opportunities, and recognizing and accepting your imperfections. If you're able to do those things, you'll be more comfortable with taking risks.

"What's the worst that could happen?" Anxiety and panic are rooted in feeling unsafe. In fact, panic attacks often stem from feelings of danger, even to the point of feeling like death is imminent. But the truth is, most of the risks you take are not going to put your life in danger.

If you're considering taking a risk, ask yourself: "What's the worst that could happen?" Allow yourself to really be honest about your worst fears and explore the potential negative outcomes of taking this risk. Maybe you do feel like your life could be in danger. Perhaps you think the risk could lead to financial ruin. Or maybe the future of a relationship is on the line.

Allowing yourself to think of the absolute worst-case scenario can help you keep the risk in perspective. After all, the worst-case scenario isn't all that likely to actually happen. Plus, imagining the worst-case scenario can also allow you to imagine how you would respond to that scenario, helping you prepare for the worst, even as you hope for the best.

"What's the best that could happen?"

Just as it's useful to think of the potential downsides of a risk, it's also beneficial to think about the potential upsides. What do you have to gain if things go well? How could that change your future? How could it help you "create happy" in your life?

The risks you take could end badly, but they could also end well. Allow yourself to envision what could go right and how it could change your life for the better. Use that information to help inform your

decision of whether or not to take the
risk.

Compare the risk to your values

The risks you take should be based on
the values you hold. You'll likely be
willing to take more risks if they could
help you reach a goal you really care
about, or support a cause you really
believe in. Realizing that the risk you're
considering aligns with your values can
help you feel more comfortable taking
the risk, as it'll help you live a more
authentic life.

"Do what is right, not what is easy."

ROY T. BENNETT

Practice

Practice taking risks. The more you practice, the easier it will get. Practice listening to your gut and following your intuition. Notice which risks you're comfortable with, and what types of risks scare you more. Give yourself permission to fail. Give yourself credit for trying.

Managing risks in a smart way

"I don't believe in taking unnecessary risks, but a life without risk isn't worth living."

CHARLES LINDBERGH

Getting comfortable taking risks is important, but it's also important to take risks in a smart way. Remember: risk matters, but security does, too.

Here are some quick tips for making sure you're managing your risks intelligently.

Understand the risk. Do research. Get informed. Don't jump into something blindly. (If there's financial risk, assess your finances. If you're basing your decision on certain information, make sure that information is valid. And so on.)

Don't take risks for the wrong reasons (reasons that don't align with your values).

Be clear headed when you decide to take a risk (e.g. not under the influence of alcohol, not in an emotionally-compromised state, etc.).

Accept input from experts, friends, or family members you trust.

Have a backup plan.

If the potential reward doesn't really matter to you, the risk is probably not worth it.

Be honest with yourself about any possible red flags you see.

Don't be afraid to say "no" if you feel pressured into a decision.

Getting comfortable with taking risks can serve you well in life. Risk can play a big role in helping you create happiness—in your career, in your relationships, in your personal development, and more. Be willing to take (smart) risks, and you'll open the door to the potential rewards.

Risk on!

CHAPTER 10:HAVE EMERGENCY SAVINGS (3 TIMES YOUR SALARY)

Your future self will thank you for this one.

An emergency fund is a pool of liquid money set aside for unforeseen expenses like a medical expense, car repair or even keeping yourself afloat between jobs. Having this money can be the difference between a small bump in your financial life and complete disaster in your entire life.

Give yourself some freedom and peace of mind.

5 steps to building an emergency fund

Tips to help you be ready for unexpected expenses

Having some extra funds available for emergencies is an essential component of your overall financial well-being, with enough cash to cover three to six months of expenses being a common recommendation. For many people, though, that can add up to an intimidating number — and can discourage even the best-intention saver.

But don't give up before you start! The game of saving is mostly psychological — and you can win it. Even if you're starting from zero, regularly setting money aside — even in small amounts — will eventually get you to your goal. It just takes time and a little discipline.

If you're ready to begin — and especially if you think you can't — here are five suggestions that might make building your emergency fund easier.

1. Set several smaller savings goals, rather than one large one

Set yourself up for success from the start. Rather than shooting for three months' worth of expenses right away, shoot for one month. Or two weeks. Whatever it takes to make your first goal seem doable.

Reaching that first goal can give you the motivation to keep going. Set your second goal higher — and the third even higher. By then, saving will have become a habit, and the positive motivation you're building by reaching the smaller goals will help propel you toward larger ones.

2. Start with small, regular contributions

Set your initial contribution level at a relatively small amount. That will ensure you don't stress your cash flow, making it too easy for you to rationalize

abandoning your savings routine.

Find something in your life you can live

without, or with less — trim back the

monthly coffee habit a bit. Pass on that

new pair of shoes, or one big night out.

Choose that amount — whether it's $5 or

$100 — and commit to saving it at

regular intervals: per month, per week, or

per paycheck. The key is that it needs to

become a habit, not a recurring struggle.

3. Automate your savings

Out of sight, out of mind: the easiest way

to save money is never to touch it in the

first place. Most employers provide

direct deposit, and some will even deposit to more than one account.

Set up a separate account just for your emergency fund and have your chosen contribution amount deposited automatically, either by your employer or your bank.

Use a savings or other type of account that you can't access easily, unlike a checking account. Chances are you won't miss it. And don't watch the account balance continually — that will only make growth seem smaller and slower. Forget about it and let time do its thing.

4. Don't increase monthly spending or open new credit cards

Once saving has become automatic, don't be lulled into a false sense of financial security and let spending creep up again. For example, if you gave up a new pair of shoes every month only to replace it a couple of months later with a new monthly shopping habit, you're not saving at all!

If you still have an extra $50 left over each month, maybe your savings deposit amount is too low. If you don't have an extra $50, you may be running up a credit card balance. Neither is productive. You shouldn't stop enjoying life while you build your emergency fund, but you shouldn't lose sight of its importance, either.

Having an adequate emergency fund is critical to your financial well-being. Be realistic, but try to reach your ultimate savings goal as fast as you can. That alone might make life more enjoyable.

5. Don't over-save

Or, more accurately, don't devote too much of your savings to your emergency fund.

By definition, an emergency fund is cash you can access quickly. That means you are most likely storing it in a low-yield vehicle like a savings account that is earning an extremely low rate of interest.

For that reason alone, you should stop contributing to that account once you've reached your ultimate goal. Start depositing into an account where it will start earning money on its own — ideally, your retirement accounts, where time will enable it to bear the most fruit.

Balancing debt and your emergency fund

If you are in the process of paying off high-interest loans or credit cards, be sure to balance your desire to accumulate an emergency fund with your need to get out of debt.

It's important to save for emergencies, but every day that you're still in debt is costing you money. What you're saving in one account could end up being cancelled out by the interest you're being charged in the other.

Instead, you may want to set a more modest emergency fund goal at the start and put any additional amount you can toward your debt. Once that's retired, you can accelerate your emergency fund savings and raise that goal. In the meantime, having a small cushion is better than having no cushion at all.

CHAPTER 11: GET TO KNOW YOUR INVESTMENTS

It's entirely possible that what you have now may have been the best policy available at the time.

But times change and so do your needs.

Is your investment really keeping up?

Better, cheaper, higher-returning options now exist.

What was right for you 5, 10, 15 or even 20 years ago might not be serving you so well now.

Which leads me into my final tip

Monetary Navigating in the Current Economy: Ten Things to Consider Before You Make Investing Decisions Contribute Wisely: An Introduction to Mutual Funds. This distribution makes sense of the essentials of shared reserve financial planning, how shared reserves work, what variables to consider prior to money management, and how to keep away from normal entanglements.

Monetary Navigating in the Current Economy: Ten Things to Consider Before You Make Investing Decisions Given ongoing business sector occasions, you might be puzzling over whether you ought to make changes to your speculation portfolio. The SEC's Office of Investor Education and Advocacy is worried that a few financial backers, including deal trackers and sleeping cushion stuffers, are pursuing quick speculation choices disregarding their drawn out monetary objectives. While we can't let you know how to deal with your speculation portfolio during an unpredictable market, we are giving this Investor Alert to give you the devices to pursue an educated choice. Before you pursue any choice, think about these areas of significance:

1. Draw an individual monetary guide.

Before you settle on any money management choice, plunk down and investigate what is happening - - particularly in the event that you've never made a monetary arrangement.

The initial step to fruitful money management is sorting out your objectives and chance resilience - either all alone or with the assistance of a monetary expert. There is no assurance that you'll bring in cash from your ventures. However, on the off chance that you get current realities about saving and effective financial planning and completely finish a clever arrangement, you ought to have the option to acquire monetary security throughout the long term and partake in the advantages of dealing with your cash.

2. Assess your usual range of familiarity in facing risk.

All ventures imply some level of chance. Assuming you plan to buy protections - like stocks, securities, or common assets - you genuinely should comprehend before you contribute that you could lose some or the entirety of your cash. Not at all like stores at FDIC-safeguarded banks and NCUA-guaranteed credit associations, the cash you put resources into protections commonly isn't governmentally protected. You could lose your head, which is the sum you've contributed. That is valid regardless of whether you buy your ventures through a bank.

The compensation for facing risk challenges the potential for a more prominent venture return. On the off chance that you have a monetary objective with quite a while skyline, you are probably going to get more cash-flow via cautiously putting resources into resource classifications with more serious gamble, similar to stocks or bonds, instead of confining your ventures to resources with less gamble, similar to cash reciprocals. Then again, putting exclusively in real money speculations might be proper for transient monetary objectives. The chief worry for people putting resources into cash counterparts is expansion risk, which is the gamble that expansion will dominate and dissolve returns over the long run. Governmentally Insured Deposits at Banks and Credit Unions - - If you don't know whether your stores are upheld by the full confidence and credit of the U.S. government, it's not difficult to find out.

3. Think about a suitable blend of speculations.

By incorporating resource classes with venture returns that drop all over under various economic situations inside a portfolio, a financial backer can help safeguard against huge misfortunes. By and large, the profits of the three significant resource classes - stocks, bonds, and money - have not gone all over simultaneously. Economic situations that make one resource classification in all actuality do well frequently make another resource classification have normal or unfortunate returns. By putting resources into more than one resource class, you'll decrease the gamble that you'll lose cash and your portfolio's general venture returns will have a smoother ride. Assuming one resource classification's venture return falls, you'll be in a situation to check your misfortunes in that resource class with better speculation returns in another resource classification.

What's more, resource allotment is significant in light of the fact that it significantly affects whether you will meet your monetary objective. In the event that you do exclude sufficient gamble in your portfolio, your speculations may not procure a sufficiently huge re-visitation of meet your objective. For instance, on the off chance that you are putting something aside for a drawn out objective, for example, retirement or school, most monetary specialists concur that you will probably have to incorporate a few stock or stock common finances in your portfolio in any event.

Lifecycle Funds - - To oblige financial backers who like to utilize one speculation to put something aside for a specific venture objective, for example, retirement, some shared asset organizations have started offering an item known as a "lifecycle store." A lifecycle reserve is a broadened common asset that consequently moves towards a more safe blend of ventures as it moves toward a specific year later, known as its "deadline." A lifecycle reserve financial backer picks an asset with the right deadline in light of their specific venture objective. The directors of the asset then arrive at all conclusions about resource distribution, broadening, and rebalancing. It's not difficult to recognize a lifecycle reserve in light of the fact that its name will probably allude to its deadline. For instance, you could see lifecycle assets with names like "Portfolio 2015," "Retirement Fund 2030," or "Target 2045."

4. Be cautious if putting vigorously in portions of manager's stock or any singular stock.

One of the main ways of reducing the dangers of financial planning is to enhance your ventures. It's generally expected sense: don't tie up your assets in one place. By picking the right gathering of ventures inside a resource classification, you might have the option to restrict your misfortunes and diminish the vacillations of speculation returns without forfeiting an excess of expected gain.

You'll be presented to huge venture risk assuming you put vigorously in portions of your manager's stock or any singular stock. Assuming that that stock does inadequately or the organization fails, you'll most likely lose truckload of cash (and maybe your work).

5. Make and keep a backup stash.

Most shrewd financial backers put sufficient cash in a reserve funds item to cover a crisis, as unexpected joblessness. Some ensure they have as long as a half year of their pay in reserve funds with the goal that they realize it will totally show up for them when they need it.

6. Take care of exorbitant interest MasterCard obligation.

There is no speculation technique anyplace that pays off as well as, or with less gamble than, only taking care of all exorbitant interest obligation you might have. In the event that you owe cash on exorbitant premium Visas, the most shrewd thing you can do under any economic situations is to take care of the equilibrium in full as fast as could be expected.

7. Consider minimizing risk.

Through the speculation system known as "minimizing risk over time," you can safeguard yourself from the gamble of putting away all of your cash at some unacceptable time by following a predictable example of adding new cash to your venture over a significant stretch of time. By making ordinary ventures with a similar measure of cash each time, you will purchase a greater amount of a speculation when its cost is low and less of the speculation when its cost is high. People that normally make a single amount commitment to a singular retirement account either toward the finish of the schedule year or toward the beginning of April might need to consider "minimizing risk" as a speculation technique, particularly in an unstable market.

8. Exploit "free cash" from manager.

In numerous business supported retirement designs, the business will match some or your commitments in general. On the off chance that your boss offers a retirement plan and you don't contribute to the point of getting your manager's most extreme match, you are missing "free cash" for your retirement reserve funds.

Keep Your Money Working - - In many cases, a work environment plan is the best method for putting something aside for retirement. Consider your choices cautiously prior to getting from your retirement plan. Specifically, try not to utilize a 401(k) charge card, besides if all else fails. Cash you get now will diminish the reserve funds available to develop throughout the long term and at last what you have when you resign. Likewise, in the event that you don't reimburse the credit, you might suffer government annual expenses and consequences.

9. Consider re-balancing portfolio once in a while.

Re-balancing is taking your portfolio back to your unique resource distribution blend. By re-balancing, you'll guarantee that your portfolio doesn't overemphasize at least one resource classes, and you'll return your portfolio to an agreeable

degree of chance.

Stay with Your Plan: Buy Low, Sell

High - - Shifting cash away from a

resource class when it is doing great in

favor a resource classification that is

doing ineffectively may not be simple,

yet it very well may be a shrewd move.

By scaling back the current "victors" and

adding a greater amount of the current

supposed "washouts," Re-balancing

drives you to purchase low and sell high.

You can re-balance your portfolio

dependent either upon the schedule or on

your ventures. Numerous monetary

specialists suggest that financial backers

re-balance their portfolios on a normal time stretch, like each six or a year. The benefit of this strategy is that the schedule is a sign of when you ought to consider re-balancing. Others suggest re-balancing just when the general load of a resource class increments or diminishes in excess of a specific rate that you've recognized ahead of time. The benefit of this strategy is that your speculations let you know when to re-balance.

Regardless, re-balancing will in general work best when done on a moderately rare premise.

10. Keep away from conditions that can prompt misrepresentation.

Trick specialists read the titles, as well. Frequently, they'll utilize an exceptionally exposed news thing to bait likely financial backers and make their "chance" sound more real. The SEC suggests that you get clarification on pressing issues and look at the responses with a fair-minded source before you contribute. Continuously take as much time as is needed and converse with confided in loved ones preceding money management.

113

CHAPTER 12:UNDERSTANDING YOUR INVESTMENTS

Be an Informed Investor

Once you have set your personal financial goals and selected a financial adviser your next step is to decide what to invest in. The same investments do not work for everyone. A registered adviser can help you assess your financial needs, goals and tax situation. They can also help you build a portfolio and recommend suitable investments for you.

Being an informed investor means never investing in something that you don't fully understand and never signing documents that you have not read carefully. Always ask the following questions before you buy:

How will the investment make money? Does it pay interest or dividends? Does it have the potential to go up in value? If so, what needs to happen for it to go up in value?

What are the total fees to buy, hold and sell the investment? Are there any penalties or fees if I have to sell the investment quickly or before its maturity date?

What are the specific risks? Could I lose
some or all of my investment?

How easy would it be to sell if I needed
my money right away?

Does the investment fit with my goals
and risk tolerance?

Working With An Adviser

Getting advice may be worth it if you are
not comfortable putting together an
investment plan or choosing investments
on your own. For example, you may not
have the time, interest or knowledge to
build a portfolio that fits your investment
goals and comfort level with risk.

Make sure you understand how your
adviser is paid and think about how this

may impact the advice they give you.

Before you invest, be sure to understand

how the fees and other costs will affect

your returns and ask about other

investments that may be suitable for you

at a lower cost.

Client Relationship Model Phase 2

The Canadian Securities Administrators

(CSA) has introduced new requirements

to ensure investors receive essential

information about the cost of their

financial advisers advice and how their

investments have performed. These

requirements are known as phase 2 of the

Client Relationship Model, or CRM2.